big c

How many giraffes are in the car?

This car is short . . .

. . . but this car is long.

sports car

Vroom, vroom!

four by four

Brrm, brrm!

pedestrian crossing

brakes

Screech!

Quick, put on the brakes!

camper van

What is Koala taking on holiday?

ice-cream van

delivery van

post van

bus

Ding, ding!

school bus

double-decker bus

open-top tour bus

mini-bus

blue coach

Honk, honk!

yellow taxi

auto-rickshaw

noisy motorbike

Vroom, vroom!

moped

tram

tram lines

tram tracks

tow truck

It's on the way to help at a breakdown.

car transporter

How many cars can you count?

pick-up truck

How many logs are there?

oil truck

recycling truck

road sweeper

What do these vehicles do?

milk tanker

heavy goods vehicle

hovercraft

ferry

Have you ever been on a boat?

fishing trawler

fishing boat

steamship

How many funnels can you count?

riverboat

water taxi

gondola

submarine

periscope

houseboat

canal boat

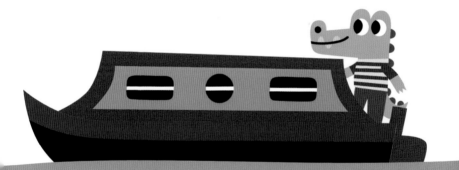

sailing boat

paddle steamer

luxury yacht

water scooter

Swoosh, swoosh!

canoe

kayak

speedboat

Zoom, zoom!

rowing boat

catamaran

cruise ship

What a big boat!

air boat

motorboat

big barge

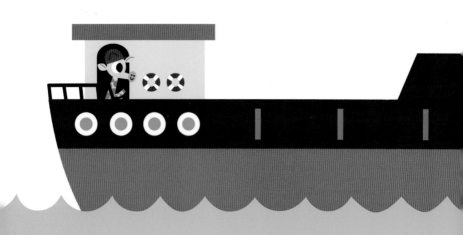

small **tugboat**

Chug, chug!

container ship

Can you count the red containers?

tanker

icebreaker

What do you think this ship is doing?

drillship

busy dumper

bulldozer

backhoe loader

excavator

concrete mixer

concrete pump truck

crane truck

giant crane

forklift truck

How many boxes are being lifted here?

loader

tipper truck

dump truck

road roller

road

The roller makes the road
flat and smooth.

tractor

trailer

How many sheep are in the trailer?

plough

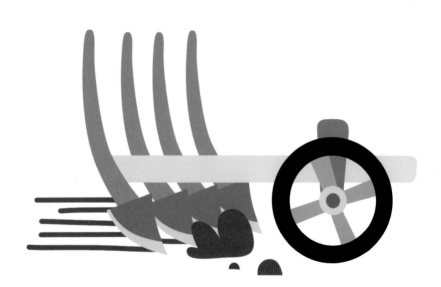

roller

manure spreader

seed drill

crop duster

crop sprayer

combine harvester

hay baler

cattle truck

horsebox

Neigh, neigh!

Choo, choo!

steam train

diesel train

long passenger train

train tracks

underground train

tunnel

monorail

high-speed train

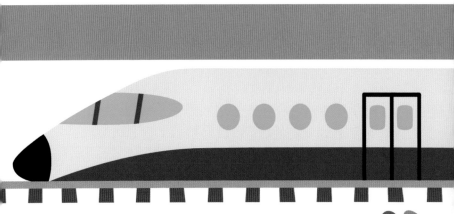

freight train

miniature railway

funicular train

Up, up, up we go!

dusty mine train

This train works deep under ground.

sleigh

What is pulling the sleigh?

toboggan

Whee!

dog sled

Woof, woof!

What colour are the dogs?

bobsleigh

How many people are there here?

snowmobile

snow plough

quad bike

dune buggy

crawler transporter

This vehicle moves rockets.

space shuttle

Zoom, zoom!

International Space Station

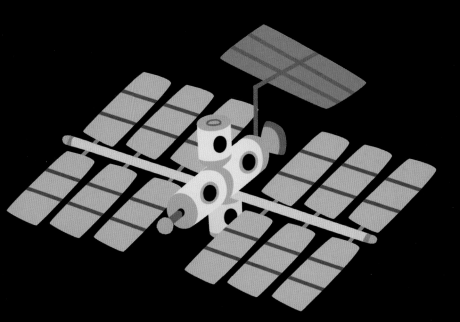

space probe

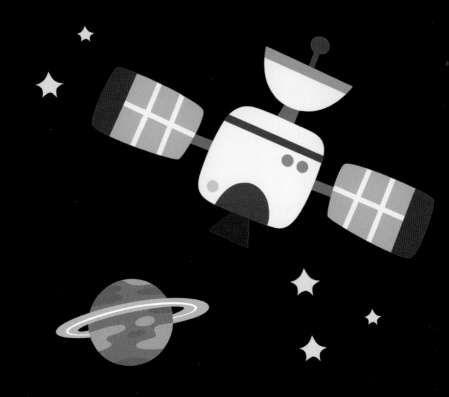

Can you count the stars?

moon buggy

bumpy craters

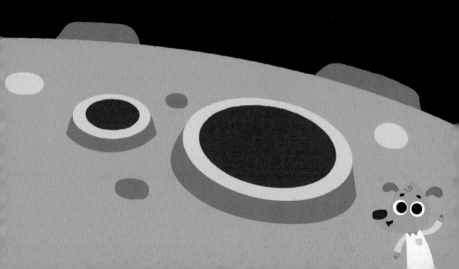

Mars exploration rover

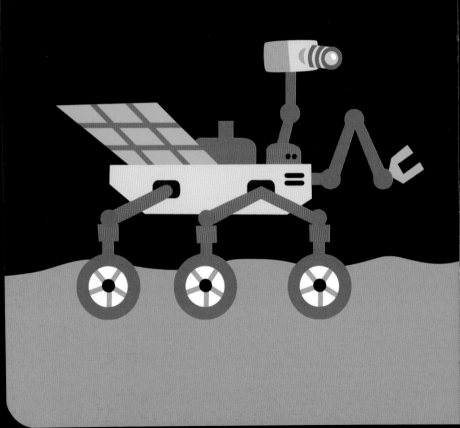

rocket

3, 2, 1 . . .
BLAST OFF!

satellite

planet Earth

red fire engine

ladder truck

hose

How is the firefighter putting out the fire?

fire

fire boat

fire-fighting helicopter

police car

Nee, naw!

Can you make a noise like a police car?

police van

police helicopter

police boat

police motorcycle

motorcycle ambulance

ambulance

air ambulance

rapid response car

mountain rescue vehicle

hospital ship

emergency rescue ship

lifeboat

life raft

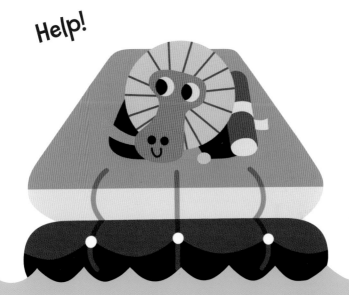

coastguard helicopter

Who is being rescued?

rescue plane

jumbo jet

four-engine jet plane

cargo plane

biplane

tow plane

glider

hang glider

airship

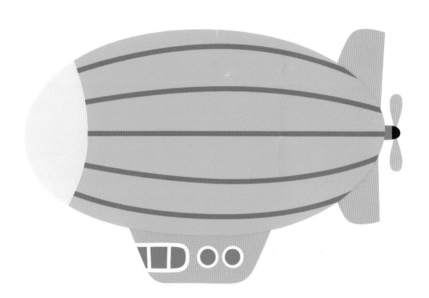

seaplane

hot air balloon

helicopter

Whirr,
whirr!

mountain bike

heavy-lift helicopter

patrol vehicle

battleship

stealth ship

aircraft carrier

military aircraft

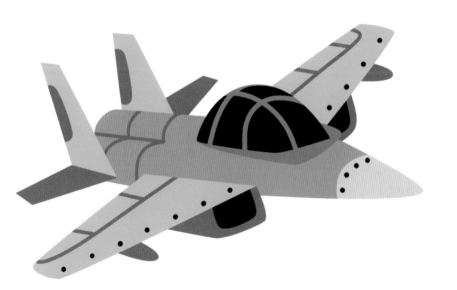

racing car

racing motorcycle

monster truck

How many cars can you count?

ice skates

rowing boat

racing yacht

dragon boat

rally car

motocross bike

scooter

balance bike

racing bike

roller skates

unicycle

tricycle

Do you like to ride a tricycle?

skateboard

surfboard

skis

snowboard

rollercoaster

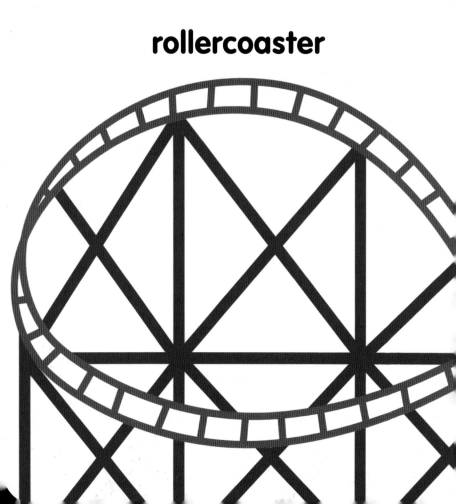

camper van

How many windows can you count?

caravan

bumper cars